GOD'S
AMAZING ANSWER
TO PRAYER

JIM BAKER

authorHOUSE®

AuthorHouse™
1663 Liberty Drive
Bloomington, IN 47403
www.authorhouse.com
Phone: 1-800-839-8640

Published by AuthorHouse 12/10/2012

ISBN: 978-1-4772-9203-7 (e)
ISBN: 978-1-4772-9204-4 (hc)
ISBN: 978-1-4772-9205-1 (sc)

Library of Congress Control Number: 2012921725

DEDICATION

This book is dedicated to my mom, dad, brother, and maternal grandfather and grandmother for spending so much time with me. Together, they helped give me a basic foundation in Christianity, ethics, love, and inventive mechanical knowledge, which has been useful throughout my life and which has helped in writing this book. I especially thank my mother for making God a priority in my life at a very young age.

TABLE OF CONTENTS

PREFACE

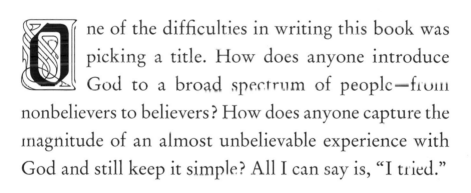ne of the difficulties in writing this book was picking a title. How does anyone introduce God to a broad spectrum of people—from nonbelievers to believers? How does anyone capture the magnitude of an almost unbelievable experience with God and still keep it simple? All I can say is, "I tried."

People usually cither believe or do *not* believe in a God, Supreme Being, or Creator, but even for those who do believe, the details can sometimes be unclear. I do not have the slightest idea of how you view God—maybe you do not even believe in God? Maybe you do not believe in anything at all, unless you can see it and touch it? If that is the case with you, you may never know God until it is too late! You may have chosen not to believe in God as of this moment, but by the time you finish this book, you should have a more in-depth and truer understanding of God than most people do as of this writing. I would hope that by offering this extra bit of knowledge, I will have helped you believe in God more fully.

God has provided me with godly information (a revelation), in conjunction with a gift that He gave me early in life, when I was a child. When I was approximately nine years old, I prayed my first major prayer to God: I prayed to Him to let me be one of the best inventors ever! In addition to inventing, God has given me a talent for mechanics, along with so much more—things you might take for granted. This includes my particular family members, the particular churches I attended, my friends, my co-workers, my schoolteachers, and still so much more!

More recently, I asked God something He has probably not done for close to two thousand years—reveal Himself! I wrote about His answer in this book. The really spectacular part of this was getting any kind of direct answer from God—but I was a little used to it by then (when I think about it), for God had spoken to me twice before.

I asked, "God, please tie all the pieces together about

You and science, and show me the total truth." God did answer that prayer, and now I feel as if He is allowing me to tell others. God expects me to do this in an orderly and godly way, giving Him respect during the process.

Many people (even pastors) have the false belief that "God may have talked to people thousands of years ago, but God does not talk to anyone in this day and age." I can bear witness to the fact that God is alive and well, and that God can and does talk to anyone He so chooses! I hope that you are as excited about that as I am.

I feel an obligation to God and to all people to explain this revelation from God in a manner that does *not* degrade God. Also every person on Earth should have another chance at getting his or her life right with God before the Second Coming of Jesus Christ *and* before death. In either case, it may not be too late for you to ask for another chance at everlasting life in the Kingdom of God—I think God realizes that many people are getting really stressed out about not knowing what to believe.

Although I use the Holy Bible for basic reference, these words are for all of humanity—all nations, all cultures. We were all created by God, so we all have the same God, whether we acknowledge that fact or not. Therefore, I've written this book for several groups of people:

- People who feel as if they are lost or as if they do not need Christianity.

- Those who believe that humans are accidents of nature; we need to save ourselves from destruction from a giant asteroid or toxic pollution; we might find life out in space, which might negate everything said in the Holy Bible; or human existence is the reason for all problems on Earth.

- Strong Christians who attended church regularly for years.

- Struggling, weak Christians, those of no faith, and those of other faiths who want and need to find God now.

- People who do not believe in God or who have only a limited belief or understanding of God.

- Those seeking to know God more fully.

- Sinners who have turned their backs on God and who do not believe in God.

- People of the Christian faith or Jewish faith who perhaps have a good understanding of God and Jesus Christ, but are seeking even more understanding.

- People who have a basic understanding of God and who want to know much more about God and how we got here on planet Earth.

This book is always timely, because no one has a clue when Jesus Christ and many from the Kingdom of God will return to Earth—it could be tomorrow, and you may need to know God really soon! You need to learn how to submit to, obey, adore, honor, love, and seek God before the Second Coming of Jesus Christ, whom God refers to as His Son, who was sent to Earth more than two thousand years ago. So we need to understand God, His Ten Commandments, and His other biblical teachings much better.

You can do this by reading this book and by attending a good Christian church that teaches from the Holy Bible, if you are not doing so already.

To have any hope of living eternally with God in His Kingdom, you need to start down the path God described in the Holy Bible, and do it soon. We are at the end of time as far as human existence on planet Earth is concerned. The final day could come 10 years, 2 years, or 6 months from now—or even today; God has not revealed the day or the hour. However, I am a strong believer that God usually tells a prophet before He takes action. God always tries to give us another chance to be saved before He punishes (and in this case, before the end of Earth).

God wants you to know Him and what He can do for you. God wants you to be able to have eternal life in Heaven—a real physical place—and also to help you while you are still here on Earth. This book is an attempt to get you refocused in life; to give you something to believe in that is fact rather than fiction, if you need it; and to introduce you to some of the almost unbelievable things in this world that you probably have not heard of.

If you do not have a clue who God is, and God is not a part of your everyday life, I hope this book reaches you especially. I recently realized that I have to try to reach *all* people while encouraging as many as possible to believe in God. This is more important than spending all of my time just trying to explain most of the revelation from God that I received. Once that is done, we can try to address more of the truth of God.

It is more important for you to get into Heaven by repenting of your sins and accepting God, Jesus Christ, and the Holy Spirit than it is for you to know all truth.

That being said, some truths and life experiences are presented in this book, along with a simple guide to becoming a Christian (or becoming a better Christian).

I respect and admire pastors and other Christian people who have made God a priority in their lives. Still, I sometimes get a little frustrated by some human opinions and misunderstandings of God. I will address some of these issues in this book. If you want to learn more about God, one thing you must remember is that pastors and churches who teach from the Holy Bible are your greatest source of Biblical teachings. You should be attending church regularly to try to understand all you can.

In almost the same breath, you have to be aware that

churches of today are not unlike the Jewish temples in the time of Jesus Christ's ministry on Earth. That is to say, pastors and church members are human, and humans try so hard to get everything so right that they wind up putting God in a box. God is limitless, and humans need to understand that principle. God can reach any person, in any situation, at any time, and can answer his or her particular need, no matter how different the person is from the status quo in our society. Accept that fact.

I will also address the notion that one of the greatest misunderstandings by humans, especially in the pastoral arena, is the idea of who God is. Many well-versed pastors slaughter scripture from the Holy Bible. I believe this can be attributed to what is taught in various seminaries today, and to the human inability to grasp certain concepts and realities of God. It is my hope that this book will help the lost, and people in the church will have new reasons to look at God a little differently, and more correctly, as they gain more insight into our real God.

I will explain why we are on a need-to-know basis with God, what Heaven is, why the Bible explains things in "Parent Mode," and how God does not contradict science. Signs and miracles, those events that we perceive as going beyond human comprehension, will also be discussed.

It is my hope that the information herein will affect you as much as it has me—perhaps even more. The knowledge that God exists might change nearly everything you do in your relatively short life on this Earth. Only with a revelation from God could we even begin to think in biblical proportions. Try to absorb and accept what you can. Try to grow at your own rate. The information in this book is meant to complement the Holy Bible and fill in voids that God purposefully left in that text, because God was not ready to reveal His mysteries—until now.

We probably all share a need to know the real truth about our existence and God's existence and how everything came to be—not just the current ideas and best guesses of our day, but the real truth. We need to be able to make any necessary changes to our lives quickly, once we've seen what really matters in life and the hereafter, before it is too late—before we die!

I hope you are as curious about God as I am. No matter how much God reveals to me, I know there is so much more to learn. It is hoped that after you read this book, you will have a greater understanding of Christianity, and you will pursue God and His Kingdom more and more with each passing day.

I am going to tell you the truth as I see it, but I will assume that some of my conclusions may not match those of others. I want you to know that if something appears to be true, whether a nonbeliever or a believer states the fact, I will give you what I believe to be the truth, regardless of its source. Although most truth about God and the Holy Bible comes from Christians, some truth comes from non-Christians who also study the Holy Bible and science. Sometimes non-Christians are able to draw better conclusions than Christians who have been taught how to interpret the Holy Bible.

It's important not to put limits on God. I assure you God has no limits! When you finish reading this book, I hope a bright light will have been turned on in your life—or, if a light is already on, I hope it glows a little brighter.

May each of you who read this book and try to comprehend be blessed beyond human comprehension.

Chapter 1:
A Little History

Before making a special prayer to God more than twenty years ago, I had studied science and the Holy Bible, and I had attended various churches regularly, for all my life. I am also an inventor; I have more than seventy inventions. Many of my inventions concerned airplanes. Although not strictly an invention, one of my favorites is my Theory of Everything (TOE), involving multiple concepts and explanations relating to gravity, magnetism, electricity, space, ether, dark energy, light, mass, energy and more.

My dad was convinced, and thus convinced me, that the path to real riches in life was to invent something that would "make you rich." So as a little boy who was

1

approximately nine years old, I had reason to pray real hard to God to "let me be the best inventor." Well, I have been inventing ever since that prayer.

One invention is a hybrid engine that runs like both a jet engine and an internal combustion engine. Star Rotor, a company in Bryan, Texas, is selling such an engine now, but I worked on this engine as a graduate student in the chemistry and physics buildings at Texas A&I (A&M) University in Kingsville, Texas. I built three prototypes of this engine starting in 1971 and carrying over to 1978.

Many of my inventions have not been released. Some have been discovered since I had the ideas, and I have the satisfaction of having had the ideas first.

When I was around nine, I had an idea for the adaptation of suspension systems for toy cars, trucks, and racers. Although I did not have the knowledge at the time to actually build the small, intricate parts, I knew how to tell someone else how I would want it constructed. I had already been helping my dad and slowly studying suspension systems under cars for a few years by then. Today, practically all toy cars and trucks have suspension systems.

The other two inventions I had back then involved a wing design and a fuselage design for airplanes. These two designs actually were incorporated years later, but again, no one had a clue that I had conceived of these designs except my mother, and she has since passed away.

When I was about twelve, I had an experience on a windy day while carrying a large piece of tin in an open area on our farm. The wind was around 30 mph, it seemed, and I was carrying the tin at my waist and straight out across (like a wing). I was amazed at how little effort it took for me to jump up high and be gently let back down to the ground.

I already had quite a bit of knowledge with small engines, including the horsepower (hp) required by different types of devices, such as lawn mowers, go-karts, small private airplanes, and outboard motors. I soon came up with numbers in my head. I then told two of my classmates what I had figured out: I could build a small airplane that would fly with a 5 hp motor, but I would double that figure and use a 10 hp motor just to have adequate power. One of these two friends said that small airplanes such as Cessna and Piper planes need more than 100 hp to fly, and if it could have been done, someone would have already done it. Well, a few years later, ultralight airplanes took to the skies! This one invention, the ultralight airplane, is probably one of the most important to me and the one that I wish I could have gotten credit for (yes, I have human desires too).

Right now, I am postponing an engine patent until I finish writing and publishing this book. I am also on hold with various new jet-engine designs and concepts that excite me. The point of all of this is just to share with you some of the ways God answered my prayer to become an inventor.

I now know that God used my whole life, up to now, to teach me a very important lesson: Always keep God the number-one priority in your life. Jesus Christ, the Son of God, said that this was the greatest commandment of all when He said, "Love the Lord your God with all your heart, and with all your soul, and with all your mind" (Matthew 22:37). I actually knew this, but we all slip at times, and I do not think that most churches emphasize this idea enough today. But I think I was close enough in getting this commandment right to get God's attention—maybe not His approval, as I hadn't given God 100 percent priority, but at least His attention.

No matter how smart or capable you are, or think you

are, God will not bless you fully until you put Him first in *all things*. Whether you are an astronaut, a teacher, a construction worker, a student, a mom, a dad, a person out of work, or whoever, you need to think about God throughout each and every day. You need to think about how your next actions can include God, and how they will affect your relationship with God. I had always heard that you should put God first, but I do not think we get enough quality training in this area.

God had given me such an unbelievable gift of an inventor's inspiration that I thought I could take it from there. I could not believe that God would give me such a gift for nothing. *He has to be blessing me,* I thought. *I must make the most of this gift, because God has blessed me so much with this gift.*

Around 1991, I had spent approximately one year building a prototype of one of my inventions. At the end of this process, I realized that I had grown apart from God, and I was completely shocked that this had happened. My spiritual wandering had not been intentional, but such a mistake can happen. In general, I have tried to put God first in my life. Decisions in my life have had to pass a "How does this affect my relation with God?" test. Temporary interference is one thing, but permanent interference is *never* okay. Even the jobs I've picked have all had to undergo the test: How will this affect my time and relationship with God? Working every Sunday, for example, was not acceptable, doing something dishonest for an employer was not acceptable, and so on. Most people have moral character like this, but it is easy to forget how to put God first when we are under so much pressure in our daily lives.

When I realized I had not put God first, I overcame my mistake by letting go a lot of the interfering interest, and then immersing myself in prayer at night; attending more church functions; studying the Bible more using audiotapes; and in general, concentrating on God more throughout each and every day.

I had spent much of my life trying to seek God and analyze God. I had tried to merge true science with God's truth and make sense of all the seemingly great disparities. I had come to a point where I felt I had figured out several of the big mysteries of God and science and creation, but I could not put the final pieces of the puzzle in place. The ultimate truth of God still remained a mystery. When I had gone as far in understanding as I could on my own, I remembered two things: God had spoken to me twice before, and then God had given me a gift of access to extraordinary knowledge, as if all I had to do was to ask for it, and then I would receive it.

I felt that it was important to experience God talking to me. Prior to 1991, as I approached the age of forty, my need for this interaction intensified. If I could only experience a vocal message being given to me directly from God, that would be the ultimate proof to me that God existed.

Well, God did speak to me! Now comes the even more unbelievable part: God spoke to me not once, but three times. The first time God spoke, the message came to me in a dream, at which point I immediately was wide awake. The message foretold what was going to happen to me—and it did happen, two months later! The second time God spoke to me, He delivered a message as if the words were projected onto the inside of the front of my skull. He delivered that message on the inside of my brain twenty minutes after I had made one of the biggest decisions in my life—a decision *for* God.

One day in 1991, I thought, *Maybe God would answer a very specific prayer.* Well, I gave Him the chance. I asked, "God, I pray for total understanding of how You, Jesus

Christ, and the Holy Spirit really fit together, and the truth about creation and science in general. I also pray for ultimate knowledge about everything—the missing link that will unlock all knowledge of You, creation, and truth. I want to understand who or what You are and how we humans came to be on planet Earth. Amen."

About a week later, I received a verbal answer from God while I was walking into my bedroom. This was the third time God had spoken to me—and this time, He literally spoke, in the form of a voice. These words, and how and when they were spoken, answered all my questions that I had prayed for. I have never revealed the words of this message to anyone. These words, the Spoken Word, meant everything to me and would probably mean little to anyone else; this exact message was for me specifically.

God answered that prayer in a way that only I would understand completely, because God designed it that way—He tailored the answer for my comprehension. Now, everything fit! But now I realized that God had not meant for me to keep the information to myself. I had to share it, and sharing it would be no easy task.

God could have given you the same message that He gave to me, yet for you it could have a totally different meaning. Our backgrounds can differ in so many ways: education, upbringing, and many, many other factors too numerous to list. God analyzes us before He speaks— that is to say that God knows our education, our thought patterns, and how each of us would interpret an answer He might give. So if God speaks directly to you, those words are to be interpreted by you specifically.

At the time, I felt that God did not want this information out yet, but He was being true to me in answering my prayer, and I am sure God had also considered the possible consequences of that answer. I believe God had, there and then, made a minor adjustment to His plans in revealing Himself: He would now reveal Himself a little earlier.

I immediately knew from within that God had given me very special information. I realized that God had given the information to me so that I might use it to further the understanding of God for all people who would listen. I also knew that if I ever were to release the information, I would have to do so in a very special and stepwise fashion. I would have to honor God, and the information would be for the glory of God and not for myself.

It has taken me more than twenty years to come up with

an acceptable way to share some of the answer that God had given me. Part of this sharing was to write the book you are now reading.

When God has spoken to me, He has communicated in very simple words and very short sentences. My first message was four words long, and then He repeated the last word. My second message was four words long.

My third and last message was three words long.

Are you thinking, *It's impossible for God to speak to someone, or for God to give so much information with so few words*? If you are wondering about things on Earth or in Heaven, or about God, do *not* be afraid to ask God! He might surprise you too.

Even if you cannot accept all you read here about my experiences, at least pick up the Holy Bible and find out all you need to know. What I present here is just another tool of truth, presented to help you understand God a little better. If the truth I present here helps you seek God more, read the Holy Bible more, and understand God more, that is great.

In addition to reading the Bible, attending church is a good way to connect with God. I have attended different churches over time. A few standouts over my lifetime include Calvary Missionary Church (during the years of 1961–1968) in San Antonio, Texas, where Frank Stribling was senior pastor. At this church, people were taught from the pulpit how to love others, from their brothers and sisters to strangers on the street; people in this church applied these teachings. Also I was blessed to be in the same church that Dr. George M. Lamsa moved to. Dr. Lamsa moved there mainly because our church was the first church that wholly accepted his Bible translation as being closer to the original meaning than any other Bible translation. Dr. Lamsa had translated the entire Bible using his knowledge and access to ancient manuscripts written in Aramaic. He also had written several other biblical books.

The Holy Bible KJV is the sixth language from Aramaic; now we had an English version, Dr. Lamsa's translation, which was based on the original meaning of the words in Aramaic. The truly amazing thing to me is that in Dr. Lamsa's English version, the meaning and the words were extremely close (almost identical) to the original English version (King James). Only the idioms in the Holy Bible differed in meaning, and that is to be expected according to Dr. Lamsa, who explained this very well. Idioms in Aramaic make no sense to anyone else except to Aramaic people of that era, but the Aramaic language has not changed for two thousand years, unlike the English language. Since Dr. Lamsa grew up speaking Aramaic, he understood the original meaning better than almost anyone else. And by obtaining his doctorate in the United States, he became very well acquainted with the English language and idioms as well. He was able to do what no other person had done so far: translate most of the idioms used in the Holy Bible that had not previously made sense. An idiom such as "straight from the horse's mouth" would have meaning to most people in the United States now, but would probably not make sense to anyone else in the world. Dr. Lamsa helped me greatly understand the Holy Bible more, possibly, than anyone else could have. I treasure the time I spent around this great man, and I treasure the time I attended this church and body of believers.

Another church I was privileged to attend was First United Methodist Church in Houston, where Dr. Bill Hinson was pastor. While I was there, this church also hosted a biblical scholar by the name of Jim Fleming, who added to my understanding of the Holy Bible in the time of Jesus Christ's ministry on Earth.

Pastor John Hagee's Church has and is helping me tremendously, mainly through its TV ministry. His church is known by the name Cornerstone and is also referred to as John Hagee Ministries, located in San Antonio, Texas. I am blessed to be able to attend this church when I pass through San Antonio. I recommend this church to anyone, for it appears to be one of the most knowledgeable churches anywhere and has an unbelievable grasp of knowledge concerning the Book of Revelation. This church also provides the most complete biblical teachings of any church I have ever seen. I highly recommend it to anyone and everyone. This church also honors the Jewish heritage through CUFI (Christians United for Israel). The Jewish people brought us most, if not all, of the Holy Bible that we Christians currently have—also, Jesus Christ, the Son of God, was born Jewish.

The church I presently attend is also providing a very good place to worship God in the presence of other struggling Christians such as myself. This church has a strong missions program. The congregants' love for one another is also one of this church's strong attributes. The Apostle Paul stated that "People should have faith, hope and love, all three, but the greatest of these is love" (1 Corinthians 13:13). We have a very loving pastor, along with his family, and this church tries to be accepting and loving toward all people who come in, just as Jesus Christ wants us to be.

I have to especially thank all of the churches I have attended over my lifetime for all the inspiration and teaching of the Holy Bible. With their help, I gained a deeper understanding of God, Jesus Christ, the Holy Spirit, and the history of God's interaction with His prize creation: humans. Yet for much of my life, I had not given much credibility to the idea that God plans as much as He does. I used to believe that any notion of God making long-range plans, such as choosing your parents or grandparents, was foolish at best. Now, I am grateful and amazed that God planned and put all of this together for me, and I encourage you to find the blessings He has in store for you.

Despite their strengths, churches may have a shortcoming. You may be surprised to learn that many churches, colleges, and seminaries teach that God has not revealed Himself to anyone since the time that Jesus Christ came to Earth. I consider this belief a human weakness that has shown itself even in churches. I believe the notion is more of an attempt to control people and keep their perceptions consistent and limited to only one main book and one main person, Jesus Christ. But if these same people read the Holy Bible enough, they would know that Jesus Christ revealed Himself years later to a non-Christian, Saul (later a Christian given the name Paul) *and* later to John, for the Book of Revelation. So you see, even the Holy Bible rejects the notion that God did not speak to anyone after the resurrection of Jesus Christ.

Approximately fifteen years ago at the church I was attending, a person in my Sunday-school class made a big spectacle by challenging "anyone in the class to give even one instance of God talking to any one of you or anyone you know." None of us raised our hands. It took great restraint and regret on my part not to correct this person then and there, for I had been working on a testimony I was to give in front of one of the largest churches in Houston, Texas, to the effect that God had indeed spoken to me—not once, but on three separate occasions.

About three weeks later, after the end of the service in which I gave the testimony, this same person walked all the way up to the front of the church (I was in the choir) and put a hand up with one finger pointing, at the same time trying to ask me a question—and then this person turned around 360 degrees in place. This entire maneuver was repeated a total of three times. The question never got out of this person's mouth, but after the third time, this person walked back down the aisle and did not return to that church while I was there. It appeared that this person could not handle the truth. Maybe this person thought, "I am smarter than all these Christians who believe in a God that they can not prove exists." This person certainly could not handle the truth that I had put forth.

On that same day, another person giving a testimony before me also revealed that God had spoken to her. This was quite amazing to me, because we were in a church that never talks about such things in public. The preacher did the talking, and we did the listening, and that was it. But this preacher recognized what had happened, and he stated a week or so after that "We are all seeing the Holy Spirit move in this church like I have not seen in years, and we should embrace this movement and not try to squelch it."

Some of the most wrong ideas come from scholars and others who are caught up in what is acceptable and unacceptable to believe and to say. My point is that sometimes you have to learn some things on your own and decide whether your observations are closer to the truth. You do this by gaining more knowledge and by praying to God for more enlightenment and for the Holy Spirit to fill you full of God's presence.

We don't live most of our lives in church, despite our desire to know God better. But we can understand more about God, Jesus Christ, and God's Kingdom when a person does a godly act. Jesus Christ meant for each of us to help others by giving them what they need at the time they need it. I encourage you to help others when they are in need.

As you come closer to God, remember that it really does not matter what your or my opinion is, if it is wrong! If there is only a slight chance that you may be wrong in thinking God does not exist, you need to study a lot more, and come to a different and more correct understanding of the real truth. It is going to be hard for many, but the effort will be worth far more than your mind can probably imagine. Remember: For close to forty years in my life, I had absolutely no positive proof of God's existence (other than feeling God's presence in my heart and witnessing what appeared to be signs and miracles), but now I have had the experience of God speaking to me three times. Use this particular experience of mine to help you believe in God, and use the information I received to help you understand our real God better.

It has been more than twenty years since God gave me the answer that revealed Him more completely. But the real lesson to learn is that God is alive and well! It is only now that I feel confident enough to start the process of teaching others about what God revealed to me, before it is too late—too late for you to ask for mercy and forgiveness and to follow God further along the path that He has set forth for you in the Holy Bible.

CHAPTER 2:
A Simple Starting Guide to Christianity

Before you start down the road of increased knowledge about God, God's Kingdom, and yourself, you need to be aware of two different mindsets, or modes.

MODE 1: If you are already a Christian, or are knowledgeable in Christianity, you should already have significant knowledge about Mode 1, which will be known here as the Original or Basic Bible Mode. I hope you are already strong in Mode 1, but if not, this chapter should help get you up to speed on a path in Christianity, and thus this Basic Bible Mode.

MODE 2:   Mode 2 is where you have to forget most of what you have learned from school, the media, the government, your family, and even the church you attend. Yes, you have to forget some of what you learned in Mode 1 to grasp everything in Mode 2, but you still need a strong foundation in Mode 1. The reason is simple: some lessons in Christianity have been taught improperly. Maybe the correct information was not available before. Maybe God did not think it was important for you to know before, and therefore that information is not in the Bible. Maybe the information was partly there, and man filled in the blanks incorrectly. Just remember: You need a strong foundation and belief in Christianity *before* you attempt to learn more about these recent revelations about God and His Kingdom.

Assuming you are a Christian already, most everything you now know is what you have been exposed to as a result of teachings from the Holy Bible. As you read on in this book, you should start understanding and knowing God a little better in certain areas. Some concepts from your previous understanding, Mode 1, may have to be modified or completely changed for you to grasp the significance of the revelations of Mode 2. If you want to learn more about God, you have to accept two major facts:

GOD'S AMAZING ANSWER TO PRAYER

1) God never has completely revealed Himself to man—at least any man that I know about; and

2) Man has had more than two thousand years since the death of Jesus Christ on the Cross and His subsequent resurrection three days later to try to understand who, what, and where God is—man still knows very little about God

Up until now, God has revealed only that which He thought you needed to know.

Although I usually refer to Mode 2 when discussing this new revelation, I have to give Dr. George M. Lamsa, a Bible translator, some credit for clarifying areas in the Holy Bible that have been misunderstood for hundreds of years. Dr. Lamsa was a walking encyclopedia when it came to the Holy Bible. In one of his teachings, he said that too many people preach from Paul's writings and "miss the mark"—miss the teachings of Jesus Christ. "They should concentrate more on the teachings of Jesus Christ," he said, "the source for Christian teachings." Prior to his arrival at our church, our preachers had indeed been teaching mostly from Paul's writings, but they soon shifted to more of those of Jesus Christ.

I agree with Dr. Lamsa: start out with the simple teachings of Jesus Christ contained in the Gospel, the first four books of the New Testament of the Holy Bible. Jesus Christ, the Son of God, made religion simple for everyone. The more man tries to examine God and His Word (the Holy Bible), the more difficult the Word seems to be to understand; this appears to be by design. You are *not* supposed to understand everything at this time! Another way to put it: Earth is your womb; you will be born into Heaven. Then you can learn much more. You are on Earth to develop in certain ways, but that development is not meant to be complete.

No matter how much we study the Bible, honoring God is also a matter of what we do. Honor God, recognizing Him as your all-powerful Creator and Father. But be a little cautious, for some people overdo the honoring of God and forget about caring for other human beings. God does not want this. God created all humans, and God wants each one of us to take care of ourselves and those around us. God wants us to take care of His creation—all of it. Many people in this day and time think this means taking care of animals and trees, and forgetting about humans. Humans are God's greatest achievement; God especially wants you to care for one another.

Refer to what Jesus Christ said about the second greatest commandment: Treat others as you would want to be treated (love one another). God wants each person to succeed and act according to God's will. That means that we are not to exclude our fellow humans from love and care. We are not to go to church, sing praises, glory, and hallelujah throughout the service, and then leave and treat people as if they don't exist—or even worse.

For example, I once considered the people working around me as close friends. When I really needed help, none of the friends I had thought I had ever helped me in my hour of need, except for one. Several said, "We will pray for you." Just before this time, another Christian friend had joined me a few times in joking about a close friend on occasion—in a good-humored way, but we were pushing the boundaries a bit at times. Well, the only person who later helped me adequately was this person we had made fun of sometimes. Boy, did God teach me something with that experience. God taught me that so many people do not know what helping others really is, no matter how much they may profess to be a Christian. If you are able to help someone who needs help, do it! Do not just pray to God for Him to do it; you do it, as you are able. Praying is really powerful, but when a person is in real need, material help from you is sometimes necessary.

Examples of material help in the Holy Bible are numerous. Remember this the next time someone asks you for help. Also, be aware that you never know what is really in people's hearts by just looking at and being around them; you have to know them inside and out.

In summary, helping someone includes both praying for them *and* physically helping them. You can do this to the best of your ability regardless of where you are on your journey in learning more about God. Even if you just opened your Bible for the first time last week, you can still help someone in a Christian way. If all you do for people is pray for them, you are approaching a state of being a lazy and cheap Christian. If all you do is give people physical help without praying for them, you are not acknowledging God's power to help in all situations. Try to do both, as you are able and as the situation calls for it.

TIPS FOR BEING A GOOD CHRISTIAN

As you grow in your knowledge of Jesus Christ, you need to take steps to support that growth.

Seek God constantly (every day) and attend a good Christian church.

Do not get too hung up on yourself, your job, your career, your hobbies, or your family. Consider using the following ideas as you support yourself on your journey.

1. ACKNOWLEDGE GOD AS YOUR CREATOR AND LORD

In general, your first step to getting into Heaven is to acknowledge God as your Creator and all-powerful God and Lord of your life—to be followed by an immediate repentance of all your past sins. You need to realize that God is aware of everything, including every big and little thing that you do. God built us, and God continues to monitor us all the time. You will never get anything past God. God is aware of everything, even things you do in secret from other humans.

Get on board with God, if you are not already, because you do not have much time. Someday, God's prophecy will come true, and Jesus Christ will return with many from God's Kingdom to completely take control of Earth in full view of everyone. (He is already in control; you just cannot see Him working.) He will punish those who have not chosen the righteous path to Heaven, but have instead done things to oppose God; God's Ten Commandments; His Son, Jesus Christ; and more. He or she who is an unrepentant and unbelieving sinner will be punished.

2. BUY A BIBLE

You will not get far in your journey without God's Word. I recommend the English King James Version or New King James Version, since these seem to be a little more faithful to the meaning of the original Aramaic text. However, newer translations may be easier to read and understand for some people.

3. FIND A CHURCH

If you do not know where to start, I would like to recommend a fantastic church that is incredible in its knowledge and teachings of the Holy Bible. This church is called Cornerstone and is located in San Antonio, Texas. The senior pastor is John Hagee, and his church is referred to as John Hagee Ministries. His services are broadcast on TV worldwide. I not only attend a church of my choice close to where I live, but I also watch John Hagee Ministries on TV to gain a more complete understanding.

Years ago I became aware that many churches' doctrines were deviating from the Holy Bible. I was developing a minor ministry that attempted to address these problems, prior to starting my main ministry. My main ministry was going to inform people about what God had said to me in His answer to my specific prayer for understanding. But a few months later, I discovered John Hagee on TV, and as far as I was concerned at that point in time, he was the only pastor getting it right.

When I found that John Hagee was reaching millions of people and doing a much better job of it than I ever could, I realized two things: I could now get on with my original goal of informing people of what God had revealed to me, and God was filling a void that I had been leaving by using someone else to correct a fair number of inaccurate and widely used teachings. Even some newer versions of the Holy Bible published over the last fifty or so years have deviated from original scriptures—and from truth, in some cases. I know of no one on planet Earth who is getting the message as right as John Hagee concerning the Holy Bible, and therefore concerning

God and Jesus Christ. Therefore I greatly recommend him and his son Matthew Hagee to help guide you in understanding the Holy Bible, and in understanding how to live a life that God and His Son, Jesus Christ, would want. I believe John Hagee Ministries can give a person the most truth in the shortest amount of time.

Information about John Hagee and John Hagee Ministries is readily available on the web. If you are blessed to live in or around San Antonio, Texas, so that you can see and hear him in person, or if you are able to hear him on TV regularly, as I do, please take advantage of this. Many other churches are fine also, but steady doses of John Hagee are good for anyone's walk in Christianity.

I won't list every church I've attended in my life, nor do I want to imply that the ones I do not recommend are no good. Basically, churches are good, and you should be attending one.

4. TITHE

You need to tithe 10 percent of your gross income to the church of your choice. This idea of a need for a sacrifice for and offering to God has been well established and documented in the Holy Bible (Genesis 28:22; Leviticus

27:30, 32; Hebrews 7:2, 4; Deuteronomy 14:22; 2 Chronicles 31:6). Tithing is also about maintaining your focus on God, all the time.

Three years ago, I had a problem with respect to tithing. The following is my true story concerning tithing; it illustrates an important principle of God.

I was more than $100,000 in debt and was slowly paying on it. But something else really bothered me: in order to pay off the debt, I could not give a 10 percent tithe to church, as I knew I should.

I basically had three sources of income: a pension check, a social security check, and a check from a small oil well that varied greatly each month and was commonly in the $700 range. I used a budget, and try as I might, I could never give consistently to the church. I had a plan to gradually increase my giving for tithing until I was up to the full 10 percent.

Well, one day about two years ago, I told myself that I had been going at this problem all wrong. I came up with a new plan that involved the following: I would now keep on giving a certain percentage from my pension and social security checks as I was able, gradually increasing them over time. My new plan would be to give 10 percent of the amount of the oil check I received; in that way, when I received more *or* less money from the oil check, it would not impact my budget so much, and I would be helping the church more at the same time, while moving closer to a 10 percent tithe overall.

I made this decision in my mind and my heart on a Tuesday. Well, on that Saturday, only four days later, I received a call that a new oil company was going to drill a new well—the start of several. As far as I was concerned, God blessed me when I made a commitment to Him in my mind and heart.

Ever since that moment, I have been blessed financially. I was instantly able to tithe 10 percent of my total income to the church, and I paid off all my debt. So you see, when I made a decision to move further in the direction God desired, even though it was perhaps not as great a move as possible, God seemed pleased and blessed me exceedingly. Coincidence, possibly, but it would be hard for anyone to convince me of that! A very important principle of God's is that He is pleased when a person starts moving away from sin and toward Him; God may even reward a person in some manner, as He did for me.

God deals with you on an individual basis; He does not

always care if you are supposedly not as pure or good as someone else. God is always working with you on where you are: Are you improving, or getting worse? Are you moving toward Him, or away from Him? Tithing is a way for us to move toward God, but if you cannot tithe a full 10 percent, start taking steps as I did to eventually reach the goal.

5. Prayer

I have recently become aware that many of us do not even know *who* to pray to. I discuss this more in the next chapter. So many of us are getting it wrong!

Jesus Christ said to pray to "Our Father," who is also the Father of Jesus Christ. Today many preachers neglect God and only pray to Jesus Christ. I can see that Jesus Christ might be displeased about this, too, based on His words about how to pray to Our Father. Many preachers lump God with Jesus Christ and the Holy Spirit, because they do not understand the truth, even though it is well defined in the Holy Bible.

A more complete and correct way to start off any prayer would be, "In the name of God, Our Father, Jesus Christ, His Son, and the Holy Spirit ..." This approach is similar to the way that Jesus Christ recommended.

Also, addressing "Jesus Christ, His Son" acknowledges that you know the difference between God and Jesus Christ. This distinction is necessary in these times, because many institutions, clergy, and laypeople call Jesus Christ and the Holy Spirit "God." It would certainly be okay to shorten this a little, as long as you keep the real meaning in your head and do not confuse other people. This is your chance to get it right and to help others understand—but it may not be the way you are being taught.

You can start with a simple and effective prayer such as the one below:

1. **In the name of God, the Father, Jesus Christ, His Son, and the Holy Spirit:**

2. **I repent of all my sins**

3. **Forgive me for all my sins**

4. **I ask for divine guidance**

5. **(You can now include other people with this basic prayer, such as your spouse, children, grandchildren, parents, relatives, extended family, and so on)**

6. **Add other requests of Your Father in Heaven as needed**

7. **Amen**

You can also pray daily the Lord's Prayer that Jesus Christ said to pray:

Our Father, who art in Heaven, hallowed be Thy name. Thy Kingdom come, Thy will be done, on Earth as it is in Heaven. Give us this day, our daily bread. Forgive us our sins, as we forgive those that sin against us. And lead us not into temptation, but deliver us from evil. Amen.

6. LISTEN TO THE RADIO

Christian radio programs are a good source of spiritual enlightenment. One of my favorites is hosted by Pastor Tony Evans from Dallas, but I also love to listen to numerous other top preachers on the radio in the morning. This helps start my day off on the right foot.

7. READING BOOKS

Another way to help you fully believe in God is to read a book of someone else's incredible experience. I would like to recommend one man's incredible true story. The book is *90 Minutes in Heaven* by Don Piper. This is a great book to read, again and again, and also to share with others.

8. Support Israel

I felt for a good part of my life that Christian churches and people therein weren't expressing respect for the Jewish people as our original source of most, if not all, of the Holy Bible. Part of pleasing God is supporting Israel and its people, who God personally selected as His chosen people, according to the Holy Bible. Again, John Hagee came through and filled that void; he is the founder of CUFI, Christians United for Israel. If you like, you can become a CUFI member.

9. Repent in Earnest

Few of the original authors of the Holy Bible had it totally together, but each of these important people documented large parts of the truth. These parts make up a giant puzzle that we humans keep trying to solve in our efforts to discover the ultimate truth about God, His Kingdom, and everything else.

One thing that should encourage you is that Paul, who is credited to have written most of the New Testament, had harmed Christians probably as much or more than anybody else mentioned in the Holy Bible. Yet Jesus Christ was able to forgive Paul and use him to glorify God. Paul had certain abilities that, when channeled in the right direction, greatly helped people to understand God.

Also, even while Paul was writing and preaching throughout many parts of the world, Paul admitted to having a sin that he could not control. God still used Paul—sins and all, past and present—to help all of us. *In this life*, God never gives up on us, no matter where we are in life, nor what we have done, as long as we first believe in God and seek Him. God forgives, but we must take the step of repentance and then ask for forgiveness. Repenting in earnest should be a daily process throughout our lives, for we are human and thus will continue to make mistakes.

Start realizing that God is real and that you are to enjoy life. You are to follow a few simple rules, including always seeking and putting God first. The fact that you are reading this book means you are likely seeking God to some extent already.

CHAPTER 3:
Understanding God More

As you employ the steps listed in the previous chapter and move between the first and second modes, you will have to understand the true identity of God, Jesus Christ, and the Holy Spirit.

When I was a child, most people were taught (and thus understood) the concept of separation, but fifty years later, people are reinterpreting the Holy Bible! You can help put the misinformed back on track.

Not knowing the differences between these three entities will not keep you from being saved and eventually going to Heaven (assuming you are seeking and obeying God as you should be). But it saddens me that anyone would teach the wrong relationship of God, Jesus Christ, and the Holy Spirit. Some people do this by calling Jesus Christ "God" and vice versa. Others forget about God altogether and give Jesus Christ all the credit; some people say God is the Holy Spirit.

Some people are getting very creative now by saying that "God, Jesus Christ, and the Holy Spirit are completely separate, but one." How confusing is that? Only humans in their limited understanding could try to make you believe such incredible nonsense.

Just realize that we humans (including myself) have not been told the complete story yet, and we have been, for the most part, incapable of putting all the pieces of the puzzle together. That is okay! Therefore, I am not going to scold anyone too badly, for such people have probably been taught by an institution that has put forth such a statement.

Who is God? Please get this right! This concept is slaughtered in many churches and in songs sang in many churches on Sunday mornings. From the previous chapter, you should already be aware of three distinct entities: God, Jesus Christ, and the Holy Spirit. In the Holy Bible (Matthew 12:31), Jesus said that you could blaspheme against God and Jesus, but never the Holy Spirit. This is a key verse that points to the separation of the three entities; Jesus Christ would not waste His time on this subject if God, Jesus, and the Holy Spirit were all the same. In another passage (Matthew 6:9), when Jesus explains how to pray the Lord's Prayer (introduced in the previous chapter), Jesus says to start with "Our Father." Jesus does not tell us to pray to Jesus Christ, but rather to His Father.

You should know that Jesus Christ is not God. This is not heresy, in spite of what many church people might want you to think! Christians are supposed to follow the teachings of Jesus Christ, but on this one, many people refer to one or two verses in one part of the Holy Bible, even though these verses contradict many other verses spoken by Jesus Christ Himself as recorded in the Gospel of the New Testament of the Holy Bible. These same people do not consider the culture and the meaning of the verses of that time period.

I was privileged and blessed to have attended a church at which this concept was explained very well by a very prominent and learned man of God who had translated the Holy Bible and who had access to ancient Aramaic transcripts. This person was Dr. George M. Lamsa, and he had written several other books about the Holy Bible and the life of Jesus. He said that people today do not understand some of the verses they quote, but in biblical times, everyone knew the meaning of such verses. Now it is quite common for people to misuse verses because they do not understand some of the original idioms. So some people, even scholars, might ignore thirty or more verses quoting Jesus Christ saying that Jesus Christ is the Son of God, and then point to one verse that they translated as meaning "Jesus Christ is God." Be careful, and remember: Jesus is not God, but God's Son who was sent to Earth so man could learn about God, His Father.

Unfortunately, many preachers in churches today give lip service to this separation, but then immediately follow that statement with, "totally one, since the beginning of time to the end of time." Many pastors, seminaries, and other institutions have adopted the idea that all three are the same. They do this, I believe, for one main reason: Humans like things simple, and praying to three different entities is awkward for humans.

Getting the real truth correct in your mind will not only help you understand more about God and His

Kingdom, but also help you tell other people the truth concerning God, Jesus Christ, and the Holy Spirit.

In the Book of Revelation, Jesus described Himself as the Alpha and Omega, the beginning and the end. Some people interpret this as proving that Jesus has existed since the beginning of time, and therefore He must be God. A more correct interpretation of this would be that Jesus Christ represents the beginning and the end to all people; He is the path to your beginning and ending, spiritually and physically. The path that Jesus Christ put forth for you to follow is the same path His Father put out for you. Jesus Christ was put on Earth so you could learn more about your Father in Heaven.

Dr. George M. Lamsa, the Holy Bible translator I mentioned earlier, explained this next concept and how people get this one verse so confused. The verse that has confused many people depicts Jesus Christ saying, "When you see Me, you see The Father" (John 5:19). That was a very common thing to say and understand two thousand years ago, because fathers taught their children everything they knew. Jesus Christ was merely saying, "I am exactly like My Father, who taught me." In the United States, a similar idiom would be, "He is a chip off the old block," meaning the son is just like his father.

Jesus Christ is at the center of Christianity for people here on Earth. I am not trying to lower Jesus Christ's standing by distinguishing Him from God and the Holy Spirit, but rather trying to get everything in the right perspective. Jesus Christ has His own unique place in God's Kingdom. This idea is based on a lifetime of learning in churches and reading the New Testament, along with what I believe to be a revelation from God in the form of an answer to a prayer. Such insight comes from knowing Jesus Christ intimately. Jesus is (just as Jesus said) the Son of God. God wants us to view Jesus in this manner, and that is exactly what you should do.

In Matthew 1:18, the Holy Bible is very clear that Jesus did not start His physical existence until He was supernaturally conceived in Mary, a virgin and Jesus's mother. Jesus Christ did *not* exist before His conception and birth. In this respect, Jesus was just like any other human being on Earth. (The exact implementation of how the fertilized egg came to be in Mary, the mother of Jesus Christ, is not known.) Jesus had to grow and develop like any other human being, except Jesus had direct communication with His Father in Heaven *and* angels tended to Him on various occasions. Also, the Holy Spirit came down upon Him, as recorded in the Holy Bible.

After His life on Earth, Jesus was raised from the dead and was put in charge of Earth and all of its inhabitants as a reward from God to His Son for Jesus's dedication to His Father's wishes. Jesus had earned this reward by showing great leadership and servanthood in teaching humans about His Father, God, while on Earth, and by enduring an extraordinarily painful death on the cross, which God had known would happen.

It is important to note that while Jesus was still in human form, God gave Him the power to heal, knowledge beyond human understanding, and other capabilities not found in humans. These supernatural powers were seen and documented mostly *after* Jesus Christ was baptized by John the Baptist and was subsequently anointed by the Holy Spirit—so, before the birth of Jesus Christ, the Holy Spirit was under the control of only God.

God, the Holy Spirit, and angels helped Jesus Christ develop into an extraordinary and powerful human being while on Earth. God and His helpers also made it possible for Jesus Christ to be resurrected from the dead.

After the resurrection of Jesus Christ, God placed Jesus Christ in charge of Earth, so it is reasonable to assume that the Holy Spirit *now* performs duties for both God and Jesus Christ. So the Holy Spirit has been under the control of both God and Jesus since the resurrection.

The Holy Bible states that Jesus Christ is seated at the right hand of God, His Father in Heaven (Ephesians 1:20, Hebrews 8:1). That means that as far as we humans are concerned, Jesus Christ is second in command under His Father, God. As such, Jesus Christ is now in control of one of God's greatest experiments: Earth, which includes you and everyone else—past, present, and future. But realize that God is still the Father—and boss—of Jesus Christ, the Holy Spirit, and all of Heaven. Though we answer directly to Jesus Christ, who is in charge of Earth, we must never forget God (His Father), nor the Holy Spirit.

Jesus Christ and the Holy Spirit are parts of God, and God existed before Jesus Christ. The Holy Spirit, as mentioned in the Holy Bible, performs specific functions for God to help humans on Earth. As such, the Holy Spirit is a very small part of God.

In summary, God rules throughout Heaven. Jesus Christ and the Holy Spirit function to serve God for humans here on Earth (dead, alive, and as of yet unborn—past, present, and future humans).

The Holy Spirit serves God and is instrumental in all communication between you and God and Jesus Christ. The Holy Spirit (sometimes referred to as the Holy Ghost) is usually referred to as the one who fills your heart, but the Holy Spirit is so much more. The Holy Spirit is continuously feeding God with information about you, and often communication flows both ways. Information is uploaded and downloaded constantly to fulfill your requests for being "filled with the Holy Spirit" and having your prayers answered. Through the Holy Spirit, God knows everything about you. A logical conclusion is that the Holy Spirit is responsible for your soul.

So Jesus, God, and the Holy Spirit are completely separate and can only be combined when we talk in broad terms about divine inspiration, godly influence, or similar concepts in which we include everything in Heaven. God's Kingdom includes Jesus Christ and the Holy Spirit, but not the other way around. If you wanted to say one term that could include everything, that term would be *God*. The term *God* could include Jesus Christ and the Holy Spirit, but when you speak of

Jesus Christ or the Holy Spirit, you have just separated out a part of God. It is sort of like saying *the United States* to represent the whole, but then referring to the state of Texas or Florida as a part of that whole.

I hope you all are starting to get the picture now that we are dealing with separate divine entities that work in harmony. God is in charge of Heaven and Earth, and Jesus Christ has been empowered by God to further accomplish God's goals here on Earth.

Chapter 4:
You Are on a Need-to-Know Basis with God

magine yourself in the military. You are given orders that you are to perform without question. You are trained well in your specialty. Your superior officers know information that you do not know, and there are reasons for you not to know.

Such is the case with God. God has put all of us on a need-to-know basis. More information would cause us to wonder about even more than we do now. Your relationship with God depends on how you perform with the information that God has given you already, and that is contained in the Holy Bible. God has put you on a need-to-know basis with everything else, and He figures you do not need to know everything else in Heaven before you get to Heaven. But right now, all of us share that status—we are all on a need-to-know basis with God.

God does not think that most of us need to know everything. Accept it! Feel good about it! And know that God is in control of everything. When God is ready for you to know more, He will be in touch.

Trying to understand God is a difficult task for humans. God chose *not* to reveal Himself throughout the history of man, which includes the recordings (the written word) of God's interactions with humans in the Holy Bible. In spite of this great mystery created by God, you are to follow God's instructions in the Holy Bible and believe in Him completely. God provided a template for us to see and know all we need to about Him; we are to simply learn about God and obey His instructions, given to us by both the Holy Bible *and* by the Holy Spirit, providing additional insight.

There are many reasons God did not explain more to us in the Holy Bible. Any scientist would understand that one does not tamper with or influence an experiment in any significant way, or the experiment will fail. God has been evaluating one of His major experiments: the creation of humans. God put humans in charge of a planet with a vast number of life forms that God also created. To God, we are tiny specks in His vast Kingdom, yet we are some of God's most prized possessions. God works with us constantly.

Every scientist has been taught and thus would understand that it is necessary to eliminate all (or as much as practical) outside influences on an experiment, so that the experiment will be valid. Otherwise it would be a useless experiment; an experiment must pass or fail on its own merit, so that real conclusions can be drawn from the results. God's experiment is nothing less than the creation of life itself, and all life forms on Earth have to be monitored continuously for any major problems, as tweaks have to be made from time to time to maintain the balance in nature that we take for granted.

In addition to this colossal experiment, God has also taken up the task of responding to many of the prayers of humans. Being one of those humans, I am going to stop elaborating at this point, because it is beyond my present capability to go much further, and because this explanation is intended to *start* you on a path of thinking from God's perspective.

We are on a need-to-know basis, and for now, we need to know four things.

1. Consider this: If the entity that has called Himself God from the beginning of time (the beginning of human life on Earth) can do everything that has been recorded in the Holy Bible, and if that entity wants to be called God—if that entity who created you and me, and who has the power to give you and me everlasting life or snuff either of us out like a candle, wants to be called God, then who are we to say that entity is not God? If that entity wants to be called God, who are we—souped-up walking computers, possibly, and expendable for sure, especially if we do not perform at least in part the way we were intended to perform—to say this entity is not God? Who are you if you doubt an all-powerful God? Those who doubt God, who do not believe in God, who dishonor God, and who turn away from God shall surely perish, as recorded in the Holy Bible (Matthew 5:29, 30; Luke 13:3, 5; John 3:16; 2 Peter 2:12). Although you may have to get used to the idea of an entirely different God than you ever dreamed of, God is real and does what He says, as recorded in the Holy Bible and as further verified by many people, including myself.

2. Part of my revelation from God involved the realization of how complicated and laborious God's work was during creation (actually, creation is ongoing for now). So before proceeding, we need to recognize that God is responsible for everything in our solar system. God did not make you directly (at least not the way humans usually interpret the word *directly*), but He did create two humans before you who were designed to keep creating humans. From this view, God is directly responsible for your creation and everyone else's creation on planet Earth. God also created a somewhat similar system for the reproduction of all other life forms on Earth. Humans have been moving closer and closer to designing massive machines that can reproduce, at least in some sense of the word. But humans have a long way to go before they can design the simplest of reproduction systems compared to what God has done. God made incredible machines—animals and humans—that are feats in and of themselves, but His feat is even more incredible when you consider that these incredibly complex machines also have the ability to make an infinite number of additional machines that are extremely similar to the originals, but not exactly identical. How incredible is that? And it appears that God is now comfortable expanding your knowledge

by giving someone (me) on planet Earth a little more information through a revelation.

3. Another aspect of giving proper recognition to God is recognizing that God is an inventor. I can understand this concept because my dad and I invented (created) many new things—although our accomplishments were quite paltry when compared with God's creations.

4. God wants you to refer to and remember Him in the image of a father—a good father who

... can dish out discipline when needed.

... loves you at the same time.

... is infinitely smarter than you.

... will take care of you.

... is patient with you.

... will teach you the difference between good and evil.

... forgives you, especially when you ask.

... who prepares you to grow up.

Jesus Christ, the Son of God, said, "You must become as little children to enter into the Kingdom of God" (Matthew 18:3). We must acknowledge Our Father in Heaven. And until we fully realize that God and Heaven are real *and* learn more about how we were created, we will probably not be ready to grasp the full physical extent of our Creator.

CHAPTER 5:
Heaven and Hell

eaven and hell are big topics, because where we spend eternity is an important consideration. Heaven is not a little invisible corner of the universe. The reason many people do not believe in God, Heaven, or hell is that they do not realize what God, Heaven, or hell is. In many human minds, Heaven either does not exist at all or is representative of life eternal, streets of gold, and the replacement of all pain and suffering with love, peace, and joy.

Most people still know so little about these entities. How can an unbeliever be persuaded by something that seems to be more of a myth than a fact? People need answers to some of their major questions now, so that their belief in God will be strengthened. God is providing answers now!

Some believe that humans are so insignificant that we are irrelevant with respect to the universe, which reportedly contains billions of galaxies. But such people do not know God. Heaven existed before our particular solar system, and it will exist long after. Our solar system is a very special place in Heaven. God protected His creation (Earth for the human species) from annihilation from asteroids and other dangers for billions of years, and God will keep on protecting the Earth and the majority of humans on it until a particular time described in the Holy Bible (Matthew 5:18, 24:35; Mark 13:31; Luke 21:23; 2 Peter 3:10). At such appointed time, this experiment of God's will be over, and God will *harvest* (keep) the good part of the experiment (the people who are trying to follow His wishes).

From a human perspective here on Earth, Heaven is a place that has no limits; it is everything God has access to, which is every star and planet—everything in the universe except for Earth and the rest of our solar system. But from God's perspective, our entire solar system, including Earth and humanity, is just another part of God's magnificent Heaven. This special part of

Heaven is treated by God like a giant laboratory for one of His greatest achievements and desires: the creation of life in His image—humans, including you and me.

Now, you have probably heard or read in the Holy Bible that Heaven has "streets of gold" and various other really nice attributes (Revelation 21:21, 22:2). What is more likely, now that we know Heaven includes everything in the universe, is that there are pockets of these extra-nice places in Heaven. These unbelievably magnificent places exist in one or more parts of Heaven, and we will be able to enjoy them for eternity if God chooses to allow us to go there. Of course, that decision is really up to us, because God has already described what is necessary for us to enter His Kingdom for eternity.

Angels and demons exist in Heaven—whoa, did I just say "demons exist in Heaven"? Yes, there are demons in Heaven; remember that our solar system is a part of Heaven. Jesus Christ taught that demons exist here on Earth (Matthew 7:22, 10:8, 12:28; Mark 1:34, 39, 16:9, 17; Luke 4:4, 8:2, 27–38). But demons may exist in "pockets" in the physical Heaven. God has allowed them to exist as long as they do not interfere with His plans. In fact, demons may exist for at least two basic reasons: 1) to suffer from punishment in a place (or places) called hell, and 2) to provide humans with temptation. Temptation is not always bad; temptation, and resistance to that temptation, builds character for some people. In those who are weak, temptation reveals those weaknesses and allows for improvement. Of course, temptation identifies the super weak people also. Eventually, God will harvest those who keep on trying to do the Will of God; the rest will go to hell. Hell is not what this book is about. This book is to help people avoid hell.

NASA (National Space and Aeronautics Administration in the United States), along with various other space agencies, universities, companies, and other institutions around the world, have been trying for years to find life elsewhere in the universe, which we now know is Heaven. All they had to do is read and try to understand the Holy Bible, just a little—maybe we could make the Holy Bible mandatory reading for multiple years in school, perhaps. The Holy Bible has more history in it than most history courses I have taken, including those in college. What could be more relevant in your life and schooling than the real history of how you got here? But for now you will have to go to a Christian school or attend church to get knowledge of this great history!

What is worse than avoiding the real history is that many people in our schools have been trying to disprove the existence of a God, a Heaven, and a hell; for example, they are pushing ideas such as "There is no judgment if you do something wrong." Anyone following this path will most likely be able to prove in time by themselves that hell is a real place.

I do not plan on spending any more time trying to enlighten you about hell—a place I do not want to comprehend, much less go to. I want to do whatever God wants, so that I am rewarded with an eternal life in a good place called Heaven, the total opposite of hell. I can only say that disbelieving people are completely misinformed and need to study many people's lives, including my own, to reverse their thinking and get back on the right track of life before it is too late.

You will find out that I am not the type of person who wields idle threats; everything I say here has been said for centuries and is well documented in the Holy Bible. The difference is that now you will be given more specific information with which to form your own ideas and opinions about real places such as Heaven and hell, and hopefully these ideas and opinions will make a lot more sense to you. Humans have struggled endlessly to try to imagine what Heaven and hell look like and where they are, but now you are a step closer to really knowing where both of these places are.

NASA, let's go explore Heaven, and schoolteachers and students, let's start teaching and discussing something you can actually see: Heaven. Heaven is no longer a religious myth or idea. We are in Heaven, and we can see Heaven stretching as far as we can look and imagine. Now, do you want to go out there? This is another way of saying, "Do you want to know God?"

Heaven is a physical place, but we also know that at our death, our physical bodies remain on Earth. Heaven is where our souls go, *if* we follow the righteous path God has given us in the Holy Bible (Matthew 10:28, James 5:20).

Think of your soul as your entire life written in the Book of Life in Heaven. More than two thousand years ago, the Holy Bible gave us the only "saved" thing earthly man could conceive of at that point in time: a book, not a computer, flash drive, or collection of brain cells (who knows what else is possible?). What is really important here is that absolutely everything you do and think is recorded somewhere in Heaven. The entire recording of your life is what we refer to and what God refers to as your soul and the Book of Life (the two are maybe one and the same, or linked—ponder that!) Another way to say this is, "Everything you have done, are doing, and have yet to do will be remembered for all eternity". After your earthly death, you will have a chance to live forever in Heaven if you are earnestly trying to obey God's commandments—if you are seeking God and repenting of your sins regularly (which are a few of the major steps of obtaining life eternal).

Now that you know where Heaven is, you need to know that all of us are very special in God's eyes. God has set aside a specific part of the Heaven for the existence and development of one of His most prized creations: humans on Earth. Earth, with its accompanying solar system and God-created life forms, was put here with humans being dominant over all other life on its surface. And remember: God made man in His image.

Besides being a special place in Heaven, Earth has been one of God's greatest experiments. Through the Holy Spirit, God is aware of everything that has happened, is happening, and is going to happen on Earth. From this perspective, you do not have to worry about the Earth being obliterated by a giant asteroid, as long as there are people on Earth who are functioning in the manner that

God intended (refer to God's Ten Commandments in the Holy Bible).

You also do not have to worry about our world being blown up or taken over, as some movies portray. Military agencies have little to worry about when it comes to this subject. Although usually such stories are officially denied, various military agencies around the world have been documented for years as having witnessed and pursued UFOs. If these agencies were extra smart, they would be trying to contact God and affirm His existence, rather than trying to contact aliens or chase them down and fire at them.

As stated before, God will keep on protecting Earth and most humans on it until a particular point in time described in the Holy Bible.

God is the ultimate judge. He gives most people years and years to get it right. Do not expect "one more chance" when you stand before God in the Judgment—He has already given you a vast number. Every second you are alive is a chance to turn your life around and live the kind of life God wants you to live. At the point of your death, God will not be listening anymore unless you have put Him first in your life.

I cannot conclude without making a few comments on a question that arises from time to time in the scientific community: does life exist elsewhere in the universe?

About the time I was finishing this book, I became intrigued by an article in *Science Illustrated* (July/August 2012, volume 5, issue 4, pages 52–61), which touched on several so-called "unknowns," including a question similar to the one above. I really wanted to comment on most of "The Universe's 10 Greatest Mysteries," but that would have steered me away from my primary goal here of honoring God and staying on message.

However, let's take a look at the possibility of life elsewhere in the universe, which I was going to comment on even before I saw this article. Since you now know that Heaven includes all stars, galaxies, and other heavenly bodies (such as our Earth) throughout the universe, what do you think God would do with such an unbelievably gigantic Kingdom?

You most assuredly would conclude that God would have other places for all types of life, including intelligent life forms like ourselves. Maybe some life forms were taken from Earth, one of God's giant laboratories, to spread life to many other places throughout the universe. Or maybe God brought life to Earth from another part of His creation.

God could not even hint in the Holy Bible that life exists elsewhere, because that would have been way beyond early man's level of understanding. Early man could not even grasp the concept of Earth as a giant spinning ball, traveling around the sun and through space at thousands of miles per hour. So Genesis had to be written in Parent Mode, which is explained in the next chapter.

CHAPTER 6:
The Holy Bible, Science, and God in Parent Mode

e humans get so caught up with trying to prove our answer to this question: "Which is right, science or the Holy Bible?"

We must realize that science, truth, and God existed long before man's idea of science ever emerged. We now have man trying to catch up with God's science and trying to call this effort "science." The Holy Bible is full of truth, science, and prophecy, but throughout the Holy Bible, men could only record what they understood in the age that they were living in. God was not ready to reveal His mystery to man in any age when man's understanding was extremely limited.

God has many tools, not just the appearance of magic and miracles, with which to get various jobs done on Earth and throughout the universe. One such tool that man has identified (and is taking credit for) is the tool of evolution, which is really a built-in adaptation tool— one of many tools used by God in the creation and development of humans and other life forms.

The Holy Bible, consisting of the Old and New Testaments, is filled with the history of man, God, creation, Jesus Christ, the Holy Spirit, demons, angels, and lots of extraordinary events. Many concepts, including creation, could not have been explained to man when man was first put on Earth. Man is still incapable of conceiving what it took to create a human being. So rather than trying to accept the fact that God created them, many people prefer to deny creation altogether.

Many people probably think it is impossible and false that creation could have taken place in six days, as recorded in the Holy Bible. Yet some people rely on the Holy Bible as a source of life guidance (as they certainly should). And other people tend to believe in the Holy Bible completely (word for word) and say unequivocally that "if the Holy Bible said it, then it is true—end of story." Still other people reject the Holy Bible because of stories that seem impossible and appear to be at odds with so-called "scientific findings."

Another option that people can believe *now* is that in some parts of the Holy Bible, information was given by God in Parent Mode.

Did you ever have a discussion about something you did not understand? How about creation? Do you think God thought it was necessary to explain every detail of how He created the stars, planets, moons, animals, plants, and humans? Of course not! God had to shift into another mode of speaking, which I will call Parent Mode. Parent Mode represents a much simpler form of communicating with someone who does not understand as much as you do. It is what a parent has to do when trying to explain things to a young child who is asking too many questions.

God does not lie. God has, however, hidden much of who He is, what He is doing, and what He did. God did this for several reasons:

1. What God said needed to be understood from the beginning of time, from man's first

placement upon Earth until the present, so God needed to speak very simply—sort of like a parent talking to a young child who is incapable of understanding the full truth of a correct answer. In this case, God speaks to His people in Parent Mode, giving utterly simple explanations to which everyone could relate.

2. God is like any good scientist performing an experiment. God's prize accomplishment, man in His image, had to develop over time in a controlled experiment. Thus, God had to limit outside influences, including complete knowledge of Himself. God did not want to influence the results of this colossal experiment.

3. God is keeping records of all the human units to see if they are performing as they were intended to function, as documented in the owner's manual for humans, the Holy Bible.

Many things beyond human comprehension, such as creation and eternal life, appear in the Holy Bible in Parent Mode. If you get this concept of Parent Mode, you will be ahead of most people in understanding some of the very basics of God's Word.

You see, science is starting to catch up to the reality of how complex creation had to be if it really happened. But the Holy Bible is still giving an explanation of creation with a Parent Mode approach, which is an ultra-simplified expression of one of God's most complex accomplishments. So sure, there is a big difference between the two explanations—between science and the Bible.

Christians can now start to give credibility to some scientific explanations that support the idea of creation, while other explanations may be guesses that appear to contradict the Bible. Informed people who understand the Parent Mode concept can start to identify some areas in the Bible that were put in simple words, versus other passages that are more exact in their meaning.

Parent Mode is especially prevalent in Genesis, where God explains how everything was created. When people realize why God and His angels were speaking in Parent Mode, they will begin to understand the Holy Bible so much more, and they won't be so offended when people compare science to written scripture, especially in the books of Genesis and Revelation.

The same concepts apply to creation. There has always been a misunderstanding of how God built humans.

God did not just breathe life into a human, as stated in the Holy Bible (Genesis 2:7); God was speaking in Parent Mode, because you do not have to know the real explanation of how He built humans in order to go to Heaven. God explained what needed to be explained in the Holy Bible, but sometimes He spoke in Parent Mode about things that were relatively unimportant with respect to entering His Kingdom in Heaven.

But with God's revelation to me, I can tell you now that God worked for a long time to make all nonhuman life on Earth, and then He made humans, which also took Him a long time to create.

When God started revealing Himself to early man, He realized things would have to be put in simple terms. Much as a five-year-old child would struggle to understand a parent's scientific explanation of life, early man would struggle to understand a deep explanation of genetics.

So you can see why God had to explain some things in Parent Mode in the Holy Bible, especially creation. This may be one of the most important things you learn from this book: always remember that God sometimes spoke in Parent Mode.

Only in the past sixty years or so have we approached a point that if we got the full explanation, we might be able to slowly start to understand.

God is so advanced in knowledge that He has to laugh at our struggles for knowledge here on Earth. Even the greatest of the scientists here on Earth are so backward and ignorant when it comes to the knowledge that God has. Yet God is ready to make incredible amounts of knowledge available to us instantly when we come into His Kingdom (pass from this life to the next). That is one reason God never emphasized knowledge as a requirement to enter Heaven. It is okay to excel in human knowledge, but do not ever let your knowledge or quest for knowledge supersede your desire for a relationship with God. Always put God first in your life—I have finally really learned that myself!

I am trying to give you more of the whole picture of the true God, His Kingdom, and His creation. Try to know God completely, as much as humans can possibly know without any more appearances, revelations, or prophecies from God. However, a few explanations may still be offered in Parent Mode and thus will be revealed more slowly.

The important thing to realize is that God is real. Do

not get too hung up if you cannot come to grips with new scientific findings or church-approved explanations of God and how you got here. The important thing is to acknowledge God and to seek Him throughout your life, including regular prayer. Honor God above all things.

CHAPTER 7:
Signs and Miracles

God does speak to people as ordinary as you and me. He can give you the same message He gives me, but we each will understand it differently because of our backgrounds, education, and other factors that make us unique. So when God gives a message, it means something specific to the receiver.

We all need to sharpen our skills so we can recognize God's signs and signals. Often I use one particular technique to identify a signal from God. God apparently knows that I respond better to this type of signal. For me, when statistics go against coincidence, that gets my attention; God knows this, for He has gotten my attention several times in my life with this technique—I am convinced.

When I was around twenty years old, I was in three car accidents within ten days, after having been involved in only one minor accident (hitting an animal on the road at night) since birth; I felt that someone was trying to tell me something this time! I felt that God was trying to tell me that I should not put all of my attention toward working on fast cars and the like, and that this was a message for me to slow down and concentrate on God more. In other words, I could be gone in an instant! Believe me, I got the message!

For someone else, one accident might have been all that was needed for him or her to get the message, but I am a scientific and mathematical person and need absolute statistical proof to believe in something, and God knows that. One wreck would have seemed possible; and two wrecks could have happened according to my calculating, statistically oriented mind. But three wrecks would have been almost impossible—more of a paranormal, godly event!

I took it as a message from God to slow down in my search for worldly happiness and devote more of my appreciation to God. My devotion to God had been strong since birth, but I have to think that God wanted me to put Him first in every way. If anyone is wondering, I was a passenger in the first wreck, and the driver who was stopped at a red light in the second wreck only four hours later. A few days later, I was the driver hanging onto the handlebars and doing a wheelie on a runaway motorcycle in the third wreck (spill). I had to choose between hitting a brick building or a light pole in downtown San Antonio during rush-hour traffic. I chose to pull the bike over on its side, since I did not like those other two choices!

Seemingly impossible occurrences are often signs from God, ways of getting your attention. I remember the first sign I saw, at about the age of six. It was a unique cloud that was all by itself. This cloud did not just have rain falling from it; it had a very unique presentation that I felt had to be a sign from God. You may think it is silly, but to me, this cloud was like a beautiful message from God. Water flowed from it sideways and rounded down, just as in the picture of a waterfall that hung in my dad's stepmom's front room.

Now, you may think this is hyperbole, but years later, God used rainbows to get my attention time after time. God did impossible things with rainbows to get my attention around the year 1990 and a few years later. I have had physics training in how rainbows are formed by light going in one side of a drop of water, reflecting off the inside of the drop a couple of times, and then exiting, and so on. But nothing or no one has ever explained how the next two stories could have happened, except by godly intervention. What I am going to reveal is impossible by human logic and human scientific knowledge, but here goes.

I was in my car driving to work in Houston, Texas, and had just gotten off the freeway. My dad had always talked and kidded about "the pot of gold at the end of a rainbow." I was with God in spirit, since my morning drive to work was commonly my close time with God. Well, this particular morning, I drove for about a fourth of a mile immersed in the end of a rainbow. Not only that, but a golden color within the rainbow extended down onto my left fender while I drove at about 35 mph. That was beautiful and magical—and godly. Even more amazing is that the car was on a road that also had a slight curve on it, yet the rainbow with the gold color stayed exactly on my left front fender for approximately a quarter of a mile, including the curve. That was a godly event—nobody can tell me differently.

Another time, a few years later, I was driving on Highway 59 at the bypass intersection outside of Victoria, Texas. God was playing with me again; actually, I think God was providing me with another beautiful experience. I saw this complete rainbow, and it was very unique. The rainbow was very strong and rich in colors, and this perfect arch was located out in a field close to the overpass that I would have to go over.

I thought, *How neat it would be if I could drive through such a rainbow—and it would be even neater if it were perfectly centered over the overpass when I went over it.* This rainbow was probably 300 to 600 feet, tip to tip, as the crow flies. At this intersection, you have to go left and then make a half circle, at which point you are heading across the overpass of Highway 59, which puts you on the bypass. Well, lo and behold, the closer I got to the top of the overpass, the more the rainbow moved until it was perfectly centered as an arch across the overpass, until I drove my car over the overpass and through the rainbow! You would not believe how blessed I felt at that moment to have been a part of such a beautiful event. Again, no one can tell me that that was not a godly event. I felt blessed by these events, but I feel even more blessed now that I can share these experiences with you.

God also gives us signs when He answers our prayers. One such astounding blessing occurred about seven years ago, when I turned over to God the task of choosing a wife; one week later, I met my future wife. Another blessing was a recent answer to prayer from many in the form of the healing of cancer. Still another was a financial blessing from God when I chose to pray for specific help in making the right decisions in an area that I could not handle on my own; God led me in the right direction, and the right decision was made. Also, when I chose to bless God with more financial gifts to the church in spite of my financial circumstances, God again blessed me financially less than a week later.

God showed me time and time again that I needed to quit relying as much on myself and to turn more things over to Him; all I had to do was ask. I still believe in being an independent person when it comes to making my way in life, but God is 100 percent a part of those "independent decisions" now.

You could say that all of these events are signs that God exists and He cares for us. God also gives us miracles, those things that we cannot explain—those things that surpass human understanding. Knowing a fair amount of science and also thinking I know about our God as well, I can tell you that miracles are simply a much higher order of science than most humans can imagine. If you knew the science behind miracles, you would not call them miracles!

Miracles are usually events that we perceive to be beyond human comprehension. This can include events that could technically happen, but which are so unlikely to happen that they defy all odds by actually taking place. You might say that a particular event could happen once in a while, but that it was a miracle that it happened at precisely the time it was needed.

I have had numerous other experiences in which God stepped in and saved my life. My dad had stated all through his life that God had saved him time after time, and I came to believe most of those statements, because I had witnessed a few of those events myself. It was often said of him, "He is an accident waiting for a place to happen." If you knew him, you would know that somebody had to be watching over him!

But this is not the time to document all of the miracles. Rather, I want to simply confirm that they happened. The Holy Bible gives instances of miracles being performed, including healing, and such documentation usually ends with a statement like, "And many more miracles were performed, too numerous to mention!" Now, I have realized for myself that it is almost impossible and really not practical to try to record every event. Thus, instead I will just note that many other miracles took place.

Maybe you have had a life-saving experience of your own. My brother frequently speaks of the time his life was probably saved when something told him to look down at the ground. He would have stepped on a rattlesnake if he had not looked down! Many times we receive signals, but we do not know where they come from. I suggest that all signals are derived from God in one way or another. The more you learn about God, the more you come to realize that God and His angels are there for you all the time.

In the beginning, God created the sun, moon, Earth, other planets, and everything else within our solar system for the purpose of providing a unique habitat for what He was going to create: one of the biggest experiments in all of Heaven (what we commonly call the universe). We humans would call that a miracle because we cannot conceive of how that could be done. We do not possess the technology, power, or brains to accomplish such a feat.

Also, you have to realize that the scientists of today are

incapable of understanding the science with which God operates all the time. God's knowledge in science far surpasses all scientific knowledge that humans have at this point in time. You can use human scientific knowledge sparingly to try to understand the Holy Bible, but now you have more truth that you can use to blend the two. As you compare some scientific knowledge with some parts of the Holy Bible (namely the Book of Genesis), you will hopefully come to a greater understanding of God's truth—the ultimate truth.

What has been really surprising to me is that a few of the most learned men on the planet who teach people about the Holy Bible have done a disservice to people, to God, and to themselves by trying to disprove many of the miracles in the Holy Bible with human explanations. We have to realize that God can do anything in any way He wants to, because God has a far, far greater understanding of science than humans. God is therefore able to make things appear as miracles to humans. As far as humans are concerned, these events are miracles, and the testament of these miracles should not be tossed away as simplistic or inaccurate. God has the awesome ability to do what seems to be impossible anywhere and at any time.

One thing I'm beginning to understand is that absolutely nothing is impossible for God. In fact, I even want to say that God plays with us more than we can realize—that is to say that God enjoys communicating with us in various ways. God enjoys His creation, humans, and He likes to make us wonder, become amazed, and try to figure things out. I am amazed at all the different tools and signs that God uses to communicate with us. Remember: God performs miracles, those things that humans cannot understand, and you should never doubt any miracle that is recorded in the Holy Bible. The more I find out about God, the more I am totally convinced that nothing is out of the range of possibilities of God.

I have spent quite some time around a few extremely capable men of the cloth, along with others who were very learned in the Holy Bible. The amazing—and very sad—thing is that the more learned some Biblical scholars seem to become, the more they try to explain away miracles in human terms. I am appalled when I hear so-called "Biblical scholars" denying certain miracles in the Holy Bible with an inadequate and incorrect explanation that tries to take away from the power of the message that God was exhibiting through a particular miracle.

If you have some basic knowledge of the Holy Bible, you may recall that Jesus turned water into wine (John 2:3–11). Also Moses uses his staff, as God has instructed, to part the sea and to perform numerous other miracles. Trumpets are used precisely in a pattern and in a way that God has instructed, and as a result, the walls of Jericho fall down (Joshua 6:1–20). The list of biblical miracles goes on and on.

We should not be trying to prove or disprove miracles in the Holy Bible. What is important is to know that God can do anything, whether something is within our understanding or not. It is not for you to know whether you, or anyone else, can explain or verify particular biblical events. The important thing to know is that God can do anything, anytime, without limits! I cannot overemphasize this fact, and I cannot repeat it too much.

There is no better sign or miracle from God than the direct approach of God—the actual voice of God that we hear if He chooses to speak to us. Both signs and miracles are used to communicate with us as well. I received three direct signals from God. As revealed earlier, I feel that God has sent me numerous signals throughout my life, but none have the stunning impact of hearing or seeing the words of God! I refer to these incidents as God talking to me.

God commonly speaks in very simple words and very short sentences. The first message I received was four words long, and then He repeated the last word. My second message was four words long. My last and third message was three words long; these three words, and how they were spoken (delivered), offered the answer to all my questions that I had prayed for. I have never revealed the words of this last message to anyone. These words, the spoken word of God, mean everything to me and would probably mean much less to anyone else. The message was for me specifically.

Along with the words that were spoken, the one thing that really stood out in this third message was the overall feeling of pride and love from God. I can compare it to the pride and love that an extremely loving mother would show for her children; it was awesome!

Another way God communicates with us is through crop circles. The Holy Bible says, "You will see signs when the time is near and people will prophesize" (Matthew 24:3, 13, 14, 21, 30–33, 36; Acts 2:16–21). The time is near, and God is showing you His existence and His intelligence, in part, through the use of crop circles. Humans cannot duplicate crop circles. God has been making contact with us, and we have not even recognized it for what it is; we try to explain it away. Just realize that crop circles represent only one of an infinite number of ways that God communicates with us. Crop circles are, however, one of the most profound and interesting methods. Crop circles exist for quite some time after they initially appear, so it is absolutely absurd for some people to say that such circles never happened, as people sometimes do with visions and other forms of messages from God. And for the final point regarding crop circles: it does not matter who or what God sent to make the crop circles, whether He sent angels or someone else. God is in charge of sending these messages no matter who does His work, and you need to pay attention and try to learn from them!

Some of these crop circles are like artwork to awe us. Other crop circles are almost like a language with symbols, indicating an intelligent being that is trying to communicate with us in the early stages of contact. Someone on Earth might be able to decode some of these messages—I do not know—but I believe that the real message is, "I am God, and I exist! Believe in me now!"

CHAPTER 8:
Conclusion

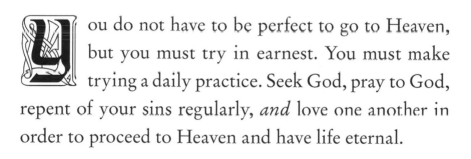ou do not have to be perfect to go to Heaven, but you must try in earnest. You must make trying a daily practice. Seek God, pray to God, repent of your sins regularly, *and* love one another in order to proceed to Heaven and have life eternal.

Some of the things I learned from God talking to me are mentioned below. I will warn you, though, that some of these things go against the teachings of many pastors and churches. I can only give you the truth that has been revealed to me through actual interaction with God. Do not be too concerned about wrong teachings in church or possibly by me; be concerned if you are not putting God first and are not trying to learn more about God.

God is a very forgiving God if you seek Him above all things!

The things I learned by experience are

- God gives prophecy (advance warning and knowledge).

- God evaluates (judges).

- God punishes and rewards (blesses).

- God is ready to forgive anything and God can forgive anything. Just ask God to forgive.

- God answers prayer in many ways.

- God is ready to bless you all the time.

- God can bless us at any time.

- God has plans for your life; pursue and fulfill those plans.

Should we be concerned with the eventual end of Earth? If you are seeking God earnestly, then no—for God is in control, and He will take care of you for eternity. If you are not seeking God, the answer is also no, because nothing you do from a human point of view can change

God's plans of destroying Earth, and you will perish along with any other nonbelievers and sinners who have not sought God, repented regularly, and asked God or Jesus Christ for forgiveness.

I do not believe I will ever write anything about science again without mentioning God; the two subjects are so intertwined. If I write another book, it will probably be a mixture of science and more revelation from God's answer to a prayer. I would also like to work on more inventions and start the process of patenting and disclosing some of my previous inventions. All the while, I plan on keeping my mind and focus on God mainly for as long as I am able, and I really want to enjoy life and all of God's creation.

Now, the time is right for you to receive a better explanation of creation and God. Hopefully, you are now a little higher up on the learning curve than you were before you read this book. God is more ready than ever to reveal His true identity. God is ready to banish sin from Earth in all its many forms. Use the guide in chapter 2 to support your growth. Always seek God, no matter what you hear spoken about Him. Know that Heaven is real and that God does speak to us in signs and wonders.

According to the Holy Bible, Earth will be destroyed at some point in time (Matthew 24:13, 14, 28:20). To properly understand why this is necessary, you need to realize that the Earth and our whole solar system was and is one mega experiment—one of God's greatest. You are one of the most advanced life forms ever created by God. God does not want to get rid of His greatest accomplishment, but God does want to take the best functioning units—the ones who obey His commandments—and spread them throughout Heaven, across the billions of stars and other bodies.